Inspirational Women of Today

Barbara Sheen

San Diego, CA

For more information, contact:
ReferencePoint Press, Inc.
PO Box 27779
San Diego, CA 92198
www.ReferencePointPress.com

LIBRARY OF CONGRESS CATALOGING-IN-PUBLICATION DATA

Names: Sheen, Barbara author
Title: Inspirational women of today / by Barbara Sheen.
Description: San Diego, CA : ReferencePoint Press, Inc, 2026. | Includes bibliographical references and index.
Identifiers: LCCN 2025005110 (print) | LCCN 2025005111 (ebook) | ISBN 9781678210861 library binding | ISBN 9781678210878 ebook
Subjects: LCSH: Women--United States--Biography--Juvenile literature | Women in public life--United States--Juvenile literature | Acevedo, Sylvia--Juvenile literature | Biles, Simone, 1997---Juvenile literature | Duckworth, Tammy, 1968---Juvenile literature | Swift, Taylor, 1989---Juvenile literature | LCGFT: Biographies
Classification: LCC HQ1412 .S53 2026 (print) | LCC HQ1412 (ebook) | DDC 305.4092/273--dc23/eng/20250331
LC record available at https://lccn.loc.gov/2025005110
LC ebook record available at https://lccn.loc.gov/2025005111

CONTENTS

Impacting the Lives of People Everywhere

Nadia Murad is a Nobel Peace Prize winner who grew up in Kocho, a small Yazidi farming community in northern Iraq. Yazidis are members of a minority group who are indigenous to Iraq and have faced religious persecution for centuries. As a young woman, Murad dreamed of opening a beauty salon in the village. But in 2014, before Murad could realize her dream, the village was invaded by Islamic State (ISIS) militants intent on eliminating the Yazidis because they do not practice Islam. The militants destroyed the village and murdered most of the residents, including Murad's mother and other members of her family.

Murad and several other young women were taken captive and sold as sex slaves. During Murad's captivity, she was bought and sold numerous times and was subjected to frequent rapes and physical abuse. "At some point, there was rape and nothing else. This becomes your normal day,"[1] she recalls. After three long months, she managed to escape and make her way to a refugee camp, where she told her story to journalists.

> **"I want to be the last girl in the world with a story like mine."[2]**
>
> —Nadia Murad, human rights activist

Since then, Murad has devoted her life to fighting for human rights. She has met with world leaders and campaigned beside other activists. In 2018 she founded Nadia's Initiative, an organization dedicated to helping victims of genocide and human trafficking rebuild their lives. That same year, she was awarded the Nobel Peace Prize for her work. She explains, "I want to be the last girl in the world with a story like mine."[2]

Paving the Way

Murad is just one of many women who, throughout history, have taken action to make the world a better place. Historically, women have had few legal rights. Among other inequalities, they have had little protection against rape or abuse, have had limited control over their own bodies or who they married, and have been shut out of many educational and employment opportunities. Nor could they own property or vote. In fact, women did not gain the national right to vote in the United States until 1920, when the Nineteenth Amendment to the Constitution was passed. Women's voting rights advocates, such as Susan B. Anthony and Alice Paul, faced criticism, arrest, and violence in their struggle for equality, but they persisted for decades. Their efforts helped transform the course of history, alter social attitudes toward women, and pave the way for modern women to take an equal place in society.

A survivor of sex slavery, Nadia Murad has dedicated her life to fighting for human rights. In 2018, she founded Nadia's Initiative, an organization dedicated to helping victims of human trafficking.

Indeed, each generation has empowered the next. For example, in 1981 Sandra Day O'Connor became the first woman to serve on the US Supreme Court. Her appointment was controversial, raising questions about a woman's ability to do the job. She worked hard to prove the doubters wrong, thereby opening the door for future women to serve as justices. Today four inspirational women—Amy Coney Barrett, Ketanji Brown Jackson, Elena Kagan, and Sonia Sotomayor—serve on the US Supreme Court, largely because of O'Connor and, later, Ruth Bader Ginsburg, forging the way. Although each of these justices has faced challenges and differs in her interpretation of the law, like O'Connor, they have all proved that women are as competent as men to serve in leadership positions.

Other inspirational women, like Madam C.J. Walker, made it easier for future entrepreneurs to break down barriers and pursue their dreams. Walker, the daughter of former slaves, faced poverty and gender and racial discrimination. By developing and marketing cosmetics and hair products for Black women in the early twentieth century, she revolutionized the beauty industry while also empowering hundreds of other women she employed as sales agents. Walker's influence is still being felt today, inspiring modern beauty industry entrepreneurs like Barbadian singer, actress, and businesswoman Rihanna Fenty. Fenty's beauty and fashion lines, which cater to diverse skin tones and body shapes, have helped make her a self-made billionaire, allowing her to generously fund several humanitarian causes.

Women Today

Social attitudes toward women have evolved over time. Yet even in the twenty-first century, women face challenges based on their gender. Even so, women all over the world are leaving their mark. Some, like Nobel Prize winner Malala Yousafzai, are well known for their contributions. Yousafzai is a Pakistani activist who spoke out against a ban on the education of girls in Pakistan and Afghanistan. In an effort to silence her, militants shot her in the head and almost killed her. Nevertheless, she refuses to back down.

Other powerful women are unheralded. They are teachers who instill a love of learning in their students, and social workers who help vulnerable people overcome challenges. They are scientists who develop new medicines and technology, and health care professionals who give hope to the sick. They are military and law enforcement personnel. And they are mothers and daughters, neighbors and friends. They are strong women who make the world a better place by their presence and inspire those whose lives they touch.

Sylvia Acevedo, from Girl Scout to Rocket Scientist

The Girl Scouts of the United States of America (GSUSA) is the largest leadership organization for girls in the world. It was founded in 1912 by Juliette Gordon Low, at a time when societal norms limited women's roles in society. Low believed that girls could do more, if given the opportunity. She founded the Girl Scouts to help girls and women reach their full potential.

Low was not alone in her beliefs, and the organization grew rapidly. According to the GSUSA, it currently has about 2 million active members and approximately 50 million alumnae. Among these alumnae are more than half the women currently serving in the US Congress, all three former female US secretaries of state, and a majority of America's female astronauts. Other influential alumnae include Venus Williams, Rebecca Lobo, Taylor Swift, and Michelle Obama, among many others.

Sylvia Acevedo is another of these awesome women. During her life, Acevedo has worn many hats. Her résumé includes rocket scientist, engineer, tech executive, entrepreneur, author, and chief executive officer (CEO) of the GSUSA. Yet her road to success has not been easy. She was often treated unfairly because she was poor, Hispanic, and female. Plus, growing up, she found herself torn between her father's traditional view of a woman's place in society and her desire for adventure and education. She recalls, "Papa never asked me what I wanted to be when I grew up, the way Mami did.

I knew he expected me to get married, have children, and keep house, just like Mami. He even said so sometimes. This made me mad, but it was just how things were."[3]

Getting a Head Start

Sylvia Acevedo was born on August 29, 1957, near Ellsworth Air Force Base in South Dakota, where her father was serving in the military. She was the second of four children. Her father was a Mexican American chemist, and her mother was a Mexican immigrant. When her father was discharged from the military, the family relocated to Las Cruces, New Mexico, where their extended family lived. Sylvia was two years old at the time.

The family moved into a small cinder block house in a neighborhood where poor, mostly Spanish-speaking people lived. Nonetheless, English was the only language spoken in the local schools. Sylvia's mother did not speak English but wanted her children to be bilingual. So she convinced Sister Diaz, a bilingual missionary working in a local church, to teach them English.

Acevedo (left) joined GSUSA when she was a young girl. She has long credited much of her success in life to the skills she learned as a Girl Scout, including eventually becoming CEO of the organization. Here, she teaches young scouts about technology.

Sylvia loved the lessons and was soon speaking English. When her older brother, Mario, started school and learned to read, she wanted to learn to read too. She almost always wanted to do whatever he did. So Sister Diaz taught four-year-old Sylvia to read and do basic arithmetic.

Sylvia became a proficient reader. In fact, when she attended a Head Start program, the teacher encouraged her to present book reports to the class for show and tell. The little girl practiced these in front of her mother, translating between English and Spanish. By the time she gave her reports to her peers, she was not nervous at all. She says that her experience as a child in Head Start gave her the confidence to speak before large groups for the rest of her life. And it made her a fervent supporter of early childhood education programs.

Girl Scouts Plan Ahead

Sylvia was looking forward to entering first grade when tragedy struck. Her nineteen-month-old sister, Laura, contracted a near-fatal case of meningitis that left her with permanent learning challenges. Sylvia's father had problems accepting the changes in Laura and became increasingly distant and ill tempered. As a result, Sylvia's parents' relationship soured, changing the once happy family. Sylvia desperately wanted things to return to normal. But they never did. Attending first grade in the local neighborhood school became the highlight of her days. Since almost all the other first graders were non-English speakers, and she was already bilingual and able to read, she was way ahead of her peers. Nevertheless, she adored her school, the teachers, and her classmates. Her mother, however, did not share her feelings. Believing that Laura might have escaped being infected with meningitis if the family had lived in a more prosperous part of the city and that the children would get a better education in another school, Sylvia's mother insisted the family move across town.

Because Sylvia came from a school with many non-English speakers, she was placed in a second-grade class for under-

Awards and Honors

Sylvia Acevedo has received many awards and honors during her life. These include the following:

- Listed in *Forbes*, one of America's Top 50 Women in Tech, 2018
- Named by *Fast Company*, one of its 100 Most Creative People in Business, 2018
- Named by Cybersecurity Ventures, Cybersecurity Person of the Year, 2018
- Awarded Hispanic Heritage Award for Leadership, 2019
- Named by *Crain's New York Business*, one of its Notable Women in Tech, 2019
- Named by *InStyle*, number seven on its Badass 50: Women Who Are Changing the World, 2019
- Named by *Forbes*, one of the Top 10 Women in Tech, 2020
- Named by *Latino Leaders Magazine*, one of its 100 Most Influential Latinas, 2020
- Awarded by Washington College, honorary doctorate, 2020
- Awarded by Duke University, honorary doctorate, 2022

performing students. Her classmates were seated by academic achievement, with the best students in the front of the classroom and the worst in the rear. As a new student, Sylvia was given the last seat in the last row. When she took her seat, a boy who had held that seat until Sylvia arrived turned to her and whispered, "Now you're the dumbest one in the class."[4]

Sylvia forced back tears. She hated her new school, new class, and that little boy. She knew she was not dumb and silently vowed that she would not stay the worst student in the worst second grade class for long. Her chance to prove herself came a few days later, when the teacher asked her to read a few sentences aloud. Rather than stopping after a few sentences, Sylvia read the whole story, and she read it well. The teacher immediately moved her to the front of the room. Even in second grade, it was not easy to keep her down.

Nonetheless, Sylvia did not feel comfortable in her new school and did not make friends until one day, a classmate invited her to join the Brownies (a section of Girl Scouts for girls ages seven to ten). From the moment she walked into her first troop meeting, she felt welcome. Soon, she had lots of new friends. But it was not just the comradery that made being a scout special for her. The Girl Scouts taught her many valuable lessons, several of which were linked to selling Girl Scout cookies.

"Through the Girl Scout cookie program, I learned how to set goals; how to break up the path in terms of achievable steps; how to make business decisions; how to give good customer service."[5]

—Sylvia Acevedo

Girl Scout troops use profits from cookie sales to pay for troop activities. To fund Sylvia's troop's activities, each girl was tasked with selling seventy-five boxes of cookies. Selling that many cookies seemed impossible to Sylvia, until the troop leader broke the goal down into small, manageable steps. The leader also offered the girls valuable salesmanship tips to help them succeed.

Heeding the troop leader's advice, Sylvia met the set goal. More importantly, she learned new skills that impacted her life. She explains:

> Through the Girl Scout cookie program, I learned how to set goals; how to break up the path in terms of achievable steps; how to make business decisions; how to give good customer service. Basically how to make my golden dreams come true. . . . Girl Scouts also taught me one of my most important lessons in life which is never walk away from a sale until you've heard no three times. That's so important because it taught me how to overcome objections. It taught me about persistence. It taught me about resilience.[5]

An overnight camping trip influenced Sylvia's life in other ways. When the troop leader noticed Sylvia studying the night

Tech-Savvy Girl Scouts Take Action

One of the most popular badges that Sylvia Acevedo introduced during her time as chief executive officer of the Girl Scouts of the United States of America is a digital cybersecurity badge. In fact, in the first six months after the badge was introduced, over eighty-four thousand girls earned it. Many have used the knowledge they gained to help others. As Acevedo explains:

> They are going to senior centers and they are teaching seniors how to make sure their wifi passwords are protected. . . . We also have some girls that have taken it even a further step and they live in the agricultural areas of America. I don't know if you know but even our tractors and combines are run by sensors. The girls are working on projects like what is the sustainability of our food supply when the internet of things gets hacked and our tractors and combines aren't useful. . . . That's because a girl has learned about cyber security and she's also learned through Girl Scouts how do you make the world a better place, how do you protect your community.

Quoted in Jessica Rosenworcel, "Girl Scout CEO Sylvia Acevedo," Federal Communications Commission, October 3, 2019. www.fcc.gov.

sky, she suggested Sylvia try earning a science badge. To do so, Sylvia built a model rocket. Getting it to launch, however, was tricky. It took the ten-year-old multiple attempts to succeed, but with each failure she learned more about physics and rocketry and became more interested in science and math. Indeed, not long after, when Sylvia's fourth-grade teacher talked to the class about going to college and showed the students pictures of Stanford University, Sylvia decided that one day she would study rocket science at Stanford.

Be Prepared

Having set this goal, Sylvia constructed a plan to achieve it. She started saving money to pay for college by doing odd jobs. And she took extra science and math classes, even though girls were discouraged from pursuing these fields. As a matter of fact, when every girl in the junior high school she attended was required to take a home economics class, she refused to go to the class. She went to see the principal and told him she wanted to drop the class and take an advanced math class instead. He eventually agreed, but only if her father signed a waiver agreeing to the change. She explains, "I refused to go every day to a class that was preparing me to be a homemaker. I was going to college, and I needed to learn things besides cooking and sewing. And that's what I told Papa."[6] He, however, refused to sign the waiver until her mother intervened.

> **"I refused to go every day to a class that was preparing me to be a homemaker. I was going to college, and I needed to learn things besides cooking and sewing."[6]**
>
> —Sylvia Acevedo

Indeed, during her adolescence, Sylvia and her father often clashed. When she turned fifteen, he insisted she have a quinceañera, a Mexican rite of passage that marks a girl's transition into womanhood and, traditionally, her readiness for marriage. Sylvia refused to take part in the event. She was more interested in studying and planning for college than finding a husband. This angered her father. He had problems controlling his temper, and on several occasions, he hit his wife. On another, he beat Sylvia with a belt when she challenged him.

This did not stop her from rebelling against traditional gender roles in other ways. For example, after the family's car broke down in the desert, leaving the Acevedos stranded, Sylvia took control of the vehicle's maintenance. Because no one in the family thought to perform basic car maintenance tasks, it broke down frequently. Even though she was far too young to drive, she took a class in basic car maintenance at a local auto dealership. She reasoned that by being prepared, she could keep her family safe. From then on, she routinely changed the oil, checked the water and tire pressure levels, and so on. "It was just as the Girl Scouts had taught me: be prepared, and you can take control of your life. Cars," she explains, "don't have to break down, and people don't have to be stranded in the desert."[7]

Ignoring the Doubters

Nonetheless, no matter how carefully Acevedo planned and prepared for the future, she could not control everything. When her grandmother died and her parents could not afford to pay for the funeral, she gave them her college savings. But she did not give up on going to college. She did some research and found that New Mexico State University in Las Cruces offered a full scholarship to qualified engineering majors. Therefore, she changed her plan: she would win the scholarship, go to New Mexico State, and study engineering. She asked her high school guidance counselor for help in applying for the scholarship, but the counselor was unsupportive. According to Acevedo, "She saw a Hispanic girl. And so, she said, 'girls like you don't go to college.'"[8] The counselor then went on to inform her that girls were not engineers.

Acevedo was undeterred. She applied for the scholarship anyway and was awarded it; but not before two professors were sent by the university to evaluate her seriousness, simply because she was a girl. Despite the doubt, Acevedo proved to be an excellent engineering student. In fact, she was the first woman to be elected president of the university's engineering honor society.

While at New Mexico State University, she participated in a summer internship program at Sandia National Laboratories, a research and development center that focuses on national security. She was the only woman engineering intern at the laboratory and was not warmly welcomed. At the first meeting she attended, for example, she was not offered a place to sit. And she was given men's overalls and gloves to wear in the lab, which she managed to keep on with duct tape. But she did not let these or other little obstacles bother her. She loved engineering and quickly proved herself. In fact, during her time at Sandia, she helped design and field-test rockets, and some of her work was included in a presentation to Congress.

Rocket Scientist and More

Acevedo received her bachelor's degree in 1975. She got a job at the National Aeronautics and Space Administration's (NASA)

Jet Propulsion Laboratory in Pasadena, California. She was now a real rocket scientist, and one of the first Hispanic women to work at NASA. While there, she contributed to the *Parker Solar Probe* mission and the *Voyager 2* mission flyby of Jupiter. Among other tasks, she created complex algorithms that helped ensure the success of both missions, and she analyzed the data that the *Voyager 2* spacecraft recorded and transmitted to Earth.

Acevedo loved her job, but she never forgot her dream of going to Stanford University. So she applied to Stanford's graduate engineering program and was admitted. She was also offered a fellowship that funded graduate studies for underrepresented groups in STEM fields. Her childhood dream was coming true. Leaving NASA, she attended Stanford, studying systems engineering. As part of her studies, she became involved in the newly developing computer revolution. By the time she received her master's degree, she was a skilled computer scientist.

Acevedo was one of the first Hispanic women to work at NASA. While there, she contributed to the Voyager 2 *mission flyby of Jupiter.*

In this 2017 photo, Acevedo assists a member of the Girl Scouts of Central Maryland build a simple robotic arm. She is focused on getting young girls interested in science and technology.

Acevedo was one of the first Hispanics, male or female, to earn a graduate degree in engineering from Stanford. Upon graduating, she became a systems engineer for IBM. While she was working there, tragedy struck. Her father, who was suffering from depression, killed her mother and then himself. She says, "It was like a nuclear bomb went off in the family."[9] Sylvia was twenty-eight years old at the time. It took years of mental health therapy for her to overcome the emotional trauma. But she did.

Over the next few decades, she served as an engineer and an executive at several technology companies, including Apple and Dell; cofounded two digital marketing firms; served on Barack Obama's President's Advisory Commission on Educational Excellence for Hispanics; wrote a book about her life; and in 2017 became the CEO of the GSUSA. She had long credited much of her success in life to the skills she learned as a Girl Scout. Serving as the organization's CEO gave her the opportunity to help other young girls and women gain the skills she believed they needed to succeed in the twenty-first century. This meant making STEM more attractive and accessible to girls. Under her leadership, more than one hundred STEM-related badges were introduced. These include but are not limited to app and game development, coding, cybersecurity, programming, robotics, space science, and weather-pattern analysis badges. She explains, "The world is changing very rapidly around digital technology. . . . We don't want girls just to be users. We want them to be the creators, the inventors, the designers."[10]

> **"The work doesn't stop. When you're a pioneer in your field, it's so important that you don't just leave a path for others to follow; you have to leave a highway."[11]**
>
> —Sylvia Acevedo

Acevedo left her CEO position with the GSUSA in 2020, but she has not slowed down. Her goal is to make the world a better place. She currently serves on the board of directors of several technology companies and is a popular speaker on cybersecurity and leadership. She also is active in the Society of Hispanic Professional Engineers, advocating to bring more Hispanic women into the field. And she volunteers her time and expertise to help needy children. She has led educational and charitable campaigns that provide books, sports equipment, eyeglasses, and dental kits to children in underserved populations across the United States. She explains, "The work doesn't stop. When you're a pioneer in your field, it's so important that you don't just leave a path for others to follow; you have to leave a highway."[11]

Simone Biles, GOAT

Gymnastics is a sport in which athletes perform acrobatic skills on the floor, beam, horizontal bars, and vault. Children often start gymnastics classes at a very young age, just for fun. If they want to compete against other gymnasts, they can advance into a USA Gymnastics (USAG) Junior Olympics (JO) program. The USAG is the national governing body for gymnastics in the United States. It supports beginner to elite-level gymnasts, including the members of the US Olympics, Paralympics, and World Championships teams. Participants in JO programs advance through ten levels as they master progressively more difficult compulsory skills. Those who reach level 10 can qualify for elite status by earning a set minimum score at a national competition. At age sixteen, Junior Elite gymnasts move into the Senior Elite division, which allows them to compete in the Olympics, World Championships, and other prestigious events.

It takes years of hard work, discipline, and commitment to become a Senior Elite gymnast. To honor these resolute athletes' contribution to the sport, whenever a gymnast introduces a new skill at a major competition, the maneuver is named after that athlete. Five skills bear Simone Biles's name. Nicknamed the GOAT (greatest of all time), Biles has amassed a combined total of forty-one World Championship and Olympic medals, more than any gymnast in history. But Biles's accomplishments go far beyond winning medals. She has changed the sport of gymnastics for the better, while facing many challenges beginning in her earliest years.

Biles has amassed a combined total of forty-one World Championship and Olympic medals—more than any gymnast in history. She has changed gymnastics for the better while facing many challenges.

A Forever Home

Simone Biles was born in Ohio on March 14, 1997, to a single mother who struggled with substance abuse. Biles was the third of four children. Because their mother was unable to properly care for the children, they were put in foster care when Biles was three. She remembers that the foster family had a swing set in the backyard. Imitating her older brother, Tevin, she would swing as high as she could then do backflips off the swing, as he yelled, "Simone, you can fly."[12] Even at that early age, she was fearless.

When the children's grandfather, Ron Biles, and his wife, Nellie, learned the children were in foster care, they brought them to

Spring, Texas, to live with them and their two teenage sons, Ron II and Adam. Little Simone adored her new home and new family. Never had anyone cared for her as lovingly. Nor had she ever had as many toys, books, and clothes. Plus, the family had a trampoline in the backyard that she played on for hours. Without any formal training, when her new brothers double bounced her, she soared high in the air and flipped repeatedly before landing on her feet. She was a tiny, bubbly, bouncy girl with lots of raw talent and upper body strength. In fact, one of her favorite activities was running up to her brothers, grabbing their outstretched arms, and doing as many pull-ups as she could.

> **"Simone, you can fly."[12]**
>
> —Tevin Biles, brother of Simone Biles

Ron and Nellie adopted Simone and her younger sister Adria in 2003. The two older children wanted to live closer to their mother, so an aunt in Ohio adopted them. Simone missed them but was very happy to finally have supportive parents and a forever home. Right away, she began calling Nellie and Ron Mom and Dad. As she wrote in her autobiography, "When it comes to how things turned out, I'm not sorry. I'm part of a beautiful family that is closer and more loving than any I could've ever chosen."[13]

Gymnastics Is Fun!

Not long after she was adopted, the day care facility Simone attended went on a field trip to Bannon's, a local gymnastic center. Upon seeing the moves the gymnasts were practicing, she began imitating them. Her natural ability caught the attention of the instructors, and she was invited to enroll in classes. Simone thought it would be great fun. So, Nellie signed up Simone and Adria for two forty-five-minute classes a week. It did not take Simone long to qualify for Bannon's USAG JO team or to advance through the skills levels. By the time she reached level nine, she was spending three hours a day at the gym and was competing and winning medals in state and regional meets. She was having fun while competing and was already dreaming about earning elite status and being a member of the US Olympic team in the future.

Training Camp

When Biles started middle school, the USAG began monitoring her performance and her potential for an elite-level career. Her status as a gymnast, however, did not impress her schoolmates. She had lots of friends but was not part of the popular crowd. Nevertheless, she was considered special in the world of gymnastics. In fact, after she won two medals at JO Nationals in Dallas and was named 2010 US Challenge Pre-Elite All-Around Champion, she was invited to attend a training and development camp at the Karolyi Ranch run by famed gymnastic coaches Martha and Bela Karolyi.

"You can't go back. The best you can do is forgive yourself, take a deep breath, and get to work . . . on the next challenge."[14]

—Simone Biles

The training was hardcore, and the atmosphere at the ranch was deadly serious. Participants drilled for nine hours a day. Impassivity, silence, and conformity were the norm. Biles, however, with her exuberant nature, remained true to herself, bringing laughter and joy to the sport. The training served her well. She qualified to compete in a prestigious meet from which members of the USA junior women's team were selected. However, Biles very narrowly missed making the team. Determined to earn a place on the 2012 team, she vowed to train harder. She insists, "You can't go back. The best you can do is forgive yourself, take a deep breath, and get to work . . . on the next challenge."[14]

Making Hard Choices

Biles was set to enter high school in 2012. She was excited at the prospect of attending high school and having all the social experiences most teenagers have. However, she was now training at least thirty-five hours a week, which left little time for social

ADHD and Athletes

Simone Biles was diagnosed with attention-deficit/hyperactivity disorder (ADHD) when she was in middle school. ADHD is a neurological condition characterized by distractibility, impulsiveness, inattentiveness, and restlessness. Although most people exhibit these symptoms at one time or another, the symptoms are more persistent and severe in individuals with the disorder. ADHD can cause emotional and behavioral problems and keep individuals from reaching their potential academically.

Interestingly, many successful athletes have ADHD, including swimmer Michael Phelps, track star Noah Lyles, football player Zach Wilson, and basketball player Brittney Griner. In fact, research suggests that the condition is more common in elite athletes than in nonathletes. Indeed, some athletes say that having ADHD is their superpower. This may be because many people with ADHD have lots of energy and can hyperfocus when they are doing something they enjoy. Hyperfocusing is a type of extreme concentration in which individuals focus so intently on whatever they are doing that they are unaware of any activity around them. People with ADHD, according to San Francisco psychiatrist Mimi Winsberg, are "very good at quickly . . . routing big bursts of energy to go after a goal and hyper focusing on it."

Quoted in Anna Medaris, "Could ADHD Actually Be a Superpower for Some Athletes?," *Women's Health*, June 25, 2024. www.womenshealthmag.com.

activities. Moreover, if she made the 2012 national team, she would miss many days of classes while traveling, which is why many elite athletes are homeschooled. It was unrealistic to think she could simultaneously go to high school and pursue elite gymnastics. Biles had to decide which she wanted more. Either way, she had to give up something she desperately wanted. It was a difficult choice, but eventually, she chose gymnastics and homeschooling.

Biles's choice allowed her to focus on her training, and it paid off. She earned a spot on the 2012 team. She was now competing in big national and international meets. And she was stunning the world with her skill, placing first in vault, beam, and floor in meets in Italy and Germany and earning all-around gold in Italy and all-around silver in Germany.

Facing Down the Haters

A year later, when she turned sixteen, she was classified as a Senior Elite gymnast and would be competing against Olympic champions, which made her nervous. Plus, there was a lot of pressure on her from the gymnastic community. Feeling the pressure, at one of her first senior appearances in July 2013, she fell off the high bar. Then, during her floor routine she injured her ankle and was pulled from the event. As she limped off the stage, she overheard the coach of a rival team saying, "She's too fat. . . . Maybe if she didn't look like she'd swallowed a deer, she wouldn't have fallen."[15]

His words humiliated Biles, who is not overweight but rather small and muscular. Her shape distinguishes her from gymnasts with long slender limbs. Their body shape gives them straight lines that add to their performance. Biles, on the other hand, must work hard to produce the same level of body alignment. Nonetheless, this was not the first time she was the victim of body shaming. She was teased about her height and muscularity all through elementary and middle school. She pretended to ignore the teasing and comments, but they stung. Over time, the support of her family and her coach Aimee Boorman helped her focus on the positive and appreciate her body shape. "I feel like I'm small and mighty and pack a powerful punch,"[16] she quips.

She proved her might in August 2013 when she earned a place on the US National Senior Gymnastics Team. She was off to Belgium to compete in her first World Championships. Once again, there was a lot of pressure on her to perform. But this time, she stayed calm, ignored other people's expectations, did her best, and had fun. As a result, she won four medals, was named the 2013 All-Around World Champion, and had a new floor move named for her. Plus, she could now get a belly ring, since she had made a deal with her mom that if she won at the World Championships, she could get her belly pierced.

Biles gets advice from coach Aimee Boorman after training on the uneven parallel bars. Boorman helped Biles to focus on the positive and appreciate her body shape.

Biles was the first Black woman to win the all-around title at the World Championships and was thrilled with her victory. Italian gymnast Carlotta Ferlito was not as pleased. She told the media that Biles's win was due to her race. Her accusation went viral. A few days later, a spokesperson for the Italian Gymnastics Federation aimed more racial slurs at Biles. While Ferlito and the president of the Italian Gymnastics Federation later apologized for the comments, the damage was done. Although Biles was bothered by the insults, she was even more concerned about the impact of racism on future generations of athletes of color. Consequently, she does not hesitate to speak out against racism. She explains, "I feel like every Black athlete or colored athlete can say that they've experienced it through their career. But you just have to keep going for those little ones looking up to us. It doesn't matter what you look like. You can strive for greatness, and you can be great."[17]

Biles went on to win all-around gold in the World Championships again in 2014 and was now concentrating on earning a spot on the 2016 Olympics team. When she earned her high school diploma in 2015, she was offered the opportunity to become a professional gymnast. This meant she could accept lucrative endorsement deals worth millions of dollars. She was also offered an athletic scholarship by several universities. However, according to National Collegiate Athletic Association regulations, professional athletes are prohibited from being members of a college team. Again, she had to make a big decision. She really wanted to go to college and be part of a collegiate team. However, going pro would secure her financial future and help support her Olympics dreams, so once more she chose gymnastics. Indeed, as of 2022 Biles's worth was an estimated $10 million, making her one of the richest female athletes.

> **"It doesn't matter what you look like. You can strive for greatness, and you can be great."[17]**
>
> —Simone Biles

Dreams and Nightmares Come True

Not surprisingly, Biles qualified for the 2016 Olympics team, where her performance was legendary. She won three individual gold medals, one individual bronze, and a gold as part of the team. Moreover, she was the first American woman in history to earn a gold medal on the vault. Team USA honored her remarkable performance by selecting her to carry the American flag in the closing ceremony. Biles was now an international sensation.

Upon returning home, she took a break from competing to cowrite her autobiography. In 2017 she began a romantic relationship with fellow gymnast, Stacey Ervin. She had rarely dated before. Ervin was her first boyfriend. Around this time the USAG was involved in a sexual abuse scandal. USAG team doctor Larry

Nassar was arrested and charged with molesting more than two hundred young women and girls at the Karolyi training camp under the pretense of providing medical care. When several girls reported the abuse to USAG officials, the officials ignored the allegations.

Biles was among the victims. At first, she refused to admit that it had happened. She says:

> I felt like I knew, I just didn't want to admit it to myself, that it had happened. Because I felt like, not that you're supposed to be perfect, but I just felt like that's what America wanted me to be—was perfect. Because every time an American wins the Olympics, you're like America's sweetheart. So it's like, How could this happen to America's sweetheart? That's how I felt—like I was letting other people down by this.[18]

She was an emotional wreck but ultimately came to terms with what had occurred. In January 2018 she issued a statement disclosing the abuse and demanding that the USAG be

A Thoughtful Professional

One way that professional athletes and other celebrities earn money is by endorsing products and companies. Endorsement contracts may require athletes to help market the product by talking to reporters, giving interviews, appearing in commercials and print advertisements, and taking part in sponsored events. In 2024 *SportsPro*, a magazine for the global sports industry, named Simone Biles the world's most marketable athlete. An athlete's marketability is based on his or her influence over consumers. Biles tops sports legends like LeBron James, Travis Kelce, and Caitlin Clark, among others. Moreover, she is the first woman to head the list.

Biles takes the products and businesses she endorses very seriously. She refuses to endorse anything that she does not personally use or believe in or that does not contribute to the betterment of society. For example, remembering her earliest life experiences, she partners with Mattress Firm because the company donates mattresses, pajamas, and books to children in foster care. Similarly, among many other endorsements, she endorses Powerade, a sports drink behind a campaign emphasizing the importance of mental health, and Athleta sportswear because it is a female-focused business.

held accountable. Her iconic status gave her power, and among other consequences, Nassar was sent to prison, the Karolyi training camp was shut down, and the USAG turned its attention to creating a safe environment for athletes. Biles helped bring about these changes. Asked about her role, she said, "I think of it as an honor to speak for the less fortunate and for the voiceless. I also feel like it gives them power."[19]

Making Mental Health a Priority

Biles returned to competition later in 2018. She medaled at the National Championships with broken toes on both feet and at the World Championships with a kidney stone. When the COVID-19 pandemic struck, she was training for the 2020 Olympics. Under the stress of lockdown, she and Ervin broke up. In 2020 she began dating National Football League (NFL) safety Jonathan Owens, whom she met online, and the two were married in 2023.

To Biles's disappointment, the Olympic Games were postponed until 2021 due to the pandemic, and spectators were prohibited from attending. Nevertheless, the eyes of the world were fixed on the renowned gymnast. The pressure was unimaginable. It, combined with the lingering emotional toll of the abuse scandal, negatively affected her mental state. She developed the "twisties," a gymnastics term for a mental block that causes gymnasts to lose control of their bodies while performing aerial moves. Biles experienced the twisties while doing an especially dangerous vault maneuver. Facing the possibility of suffering serious physical injury in her current mindset, she withdrew from the competition to concentrate on her mental health. Her withdrawal drew some extremely harsh criticism from some media pundits. Podcaster and radio host Charlie Kirk, for example, called her "a selfish sociopath and a shame to the country."[20] Members of the Russian media slandered her with sexist and racist comments. In contrast, numerous health advocates, athletes, and prominent people spoke out in support of her decision. Her actions helped focus attention on the mental health struggles athletes face and made it more acceptable for athletes to prioritize their mental health. In fact, in 2022 she was awarded the Presidential Medal of Freedom largely for her mental health advocacy. She was the youngest person to ever win the medal.

A Powerful Comeback

Biles went on to compete in the 2024 Olympics, where she won one team and two individual gold medals and one individual silver. Although female gymnasts are typically between sixteen and twenty-two years of age, she has not ruled out the possibility of

Biles went on to compete in the 2024 Olympics, where she won three gold medals and one silver. She has not ruled out the possibility of competing in the 2028 games.

competing in the 2028 games when she will be thirty years old. In the meantime, she is busy. She is an advocate for children in foster care and an inspiration to many young women. As a matter of fact, she considers inspiring future generations of young athletes her greatest achievement and her legacy. She says, "As long as I'm inspiring the next generation and having fun and just making sure that it's not all about winning but still putting a good foot forward even when it doesn't go your way, I think that's what I would want [my legacy] to be."[21]

Tammy Duckworth, Guardian of Freedom

During the 1960s and early 1970s, an estimated twenty-five thousand to one hundred thousand mixed-race children were born in Southeast Asia to American servicemen and native women. The men came to the region to fight in the Vietnam War. Most returned to the United States when their tour of duty ended, leaving their Asian families behind. Some servicemen remained in Asia rather than abandon their new families. But no matter the circumstances, life was not easy for Amerasian children. They were considered inferior and discriminated against. Some were sold into slavery, and others were forced to live as beggars on the streets. Even those whose fathers did not abandon them were mistreated. Tammy Duckworth was among the latter group. "I was not treated very well," she admits. "The only biracial children that existed in Southeast Asia at the time were children of American servicemen and native women. That was not a positive background to have."[22]

An International Childhood

Ladda Tammy Duckworth was born on March 12, 1968, in Bangkok, Thailand, to Frank Duckworth, a US Army captain, and Lamai Sompornpairin, a Thai woman of Chinese descent. Tammy's brother, Tom, was born two years later. Frank Duckworth was stationed in Thailand when he and Lamai met, fell in love, and wed. The only problem was the groom already had a wife and family in Virginia. Vowing to make things right, upon his military discharge, he went back to Virginia to get a divorce, leaving his Asian family to live with their Thai relatives.

Tammy's relatives were quick to flaunt their superiority and belittle her appearance and tall stature. Worse still, they taunted her with the prospect that her father would never return. But one year later, he returned. He got a job in Bangkok as a communications expert. The Duckworths moved into their own apartment and lived a comfortable life. Tammy went to kindergarten in a Thai school, where she learned to read and write Thai, her first language. In the next few years, she would also become fluent and literate in English and Indonesian.

Tammy's father did not stay in any job very long. Nor did the family live in one place for an extended period. In 1974 he took a job in Phnom Penh, Cambodia, moving the family there. At the time, Cambodia was engaged in a bloody civil war. In fact, the children often sat on the roof of their home watching bombs light up the sky. Their parents told them the explosives

Duckworth did not have an ideal childhood. Life was not easy for Amerasian children. They were considered inferior and often discriminated against.

were beautiful fireworks. Nevertheless, the danger was real. Two weeks before Cambodia fell to rebels in 1975, the family returned to Bangkok. A year later, when Tammy's father got a job managing an expatriate community in Jakarta, Indonesia, they moved again. They remained in Indonesia for seven years, which was the longest period that the family had ever lived in one place. But when Frank's employers sold the community to another company, he lost his job. Unable to find suitable work in Indonesia, he moved the family to Singapore. However, he did not find a job there either, and the family soon ran out of money. They returned to Bangkok in 1984, but their circumstances did not improve. Believing life would be better in the United States, the Duckworths decided to move to Honolulu. Tammy's mother, however, was not a US citizen and could not enter the country legally without the proper paperwork. So when the plane took off, she stayed behind.

Life in Hawaii

Without her mother, it became Tammy's job to care for the family. This was not easy. When they arrived in Honolulu, they were broke. Without the help of social services, they might have become homeless and food insecure, which is why as a US senator, Duckworth is a staunch defender of social safety net programs. Indeed, Tammy and her brother depended on subsidized school lunches to survive; nonetheless, they often went to bed hungry.

Making matters worse, their father's lack of employment dragged on. So, sixteen-year-old Tammy took on multiple jobs to support the family. Each day after school, she handed out flyers to tourists on the beach, earning $3.35 an hour for her efforts, and she dodged traffic in busy intersections selling roses to commuters. She also scavenged the beach for coins and bills that beachgoers dropped. And she and some local boys challenged tourists to beach volleyball games, convincing the mainlanders to bet on the game, which Tammy and her buddies invariably won. "Hustling for cash," she confesses, "became a way of life during my teenage years in Hawaii."[23]

> **"Hustling for cash became a way of life during my teenage years in Hawaii."[23]**
>
> —Tammy Duckworth

In this way, she kept the family fed and the bills paid. But between her jobs, going to school, being a member of the school's varsity track team, and studying, she was overwhelmed. Meanwhile, after more than six months, Tammy's mother finally gained permission to legally enter the United States. Almost as soon as she arrived, she took up sewing to earn money, and she pressured her husband to work as a doorman for tips. Her presence eased Tammy's burden, allowing the teen to focus her energy on graduating from high school and going to college.

In 1985 Tammy enrolled in the University of Hawaii at Manoa. Right before the first semester began, her father got a good job as a federal food inspector in Virginia, and the family moved there. This time Tammy stayed behind. She did well in college. Between student loans, grants, and a part-time job working as a waitress in a Thai restaurant, she was able to pay tuition and support herself. She explains, "Coming from nothing, this really felt like something."[24]

Duckworth earned her bachelor's degree in 1989. Inspired by the American ambassadors she witnessed helping refugees in Southeast Asia, she dreamed of becoming a diplomat. A graduate degree in international affairs could help make this happen. So she applied to and was accepted by the George Washington University in Washington, DC.

Finding Her True Calling

Duckworth moved to Washington, DC, in 1989, beginning the next stage of her life. Just as she had done in the past, she worked while attending school. In the spring of 1990, she was laid off from her most recent job. A friend suggested she join the Reserve Officers' Training Corps (ROTC) and attend basic training camp for the

Women Airforce Service Pilots

Tammy Duckworth was not the first woman to pilot a military aircraft. Women pilots have a long history in the armed forces. Over one thousand civilian women, known as Women Airforce Service Pilots (WASPs), served as noncombatant pilots during World War II. They were the first women to fly US military aircraft. They piloted every type of aircraft and in total flew more than 60 million miles (97 million km). They ferried troops and supplies in and out of combat zones and served as flight instructors and test pilots. In fact, in 1944, WASP test pilot Ann Baumgartner was the first woman ever to pilot a jet aircraft.

Thirty-eight pilots were killed while serving as WASPs. But because the WASPs were not considered an official part of the military, those killed while serving were not entitled to military burial rights. Nor did surviving WASPs receive veteran benefits.

When World War II ended, the WASPs were disbanded. In 1977 surviving WASPs were finally granted military status, which entitled them to the same benefits as other veterans. They were further recognized in 2009 when all WASPs, both living and dead, were awarded the Congressional Gold Medal for their service.

summer. Duckworth thought it would be a good way to save some money; plus, she liked the idea of the physical challenge. "That's how I made the best decision of my life—a decision that started me down the path to my true calling,"[25] she says.

She spent the next eight weeks in Fort Knox, Kentucky. Even though she was extremely fit, basic training was a challenge. But she loved it. She loved the idea of serving her country. And she appreciated that soldiers rose through the ranks based on their ability and experience rather than their racial or economic background. To fulfill ROTC requirements, she continued attending training camps for the next two years. In 1991 she met her future husband, Bryan Bowlsbey, a fellow cadet, at training camp. Like Duckworth, he was older than most of the other cadets, who were almost all undergraduate students. Bowlsbey had previously served as an enlisted soldier in the army and was a member of the Maryland National Guard when he enrolled in college and ROTC.

Duckworth and Bowlsbey dated for the next two years. In 1991 she earned her master's degree and entered a doctoral program at Northern Illinois University, while continuing to satisfy her ROTC training. Bowlsbey accompanied her to Illinois, and the two married in 1993. Duckworth earned her military commission in 1992, becoming a second lieutenant in the army reserves and later, the Illinois National Guard. Until 2015 women could not hold direct combat positions in the military, but they could serve in war zones as pilots on defensive missions. Determined to face the same danger as her male colleagues, Duckworth chose helicopter pilot as her preferred assignment. She explains, "I was going to get the same rank, the same pay, and I wanted to face the same risks [as male soldiers]."[26] Therefore, in 1993 she suspended her doctoral studies to attend flight school at Fort Rucker in Alabama for one year.

"My nation trusted me and entrusted me with the privilege of flying this amazing machine! This little Asian girl who was starving in Hawaii, they looked at me and said, 'You got potential, kid.'"[27]

—Tammy Duckworth

Duckworth loved flying the big metal birds. Out of forty students in the class, she finished among the top three. She qualified to pilot Black Hawk helicopters, which were the most technologically advanced helicopters at the time. "Can you imagine?" she muses. "My nation trusted me and entrusted me with the privilege of flying this amazing machine! This little Asian girl who was starving in Hawaii, they looked at me and said, 'You got potential, kid.'"[27]

Brave Warrior

Duckworth and Bowlsbey settled into married life in Illinois, where she worked on her PhD while fulfilling her army reserve duties and holding down several civilian jobs. But their life together was frequently interrupted. Between 1994 and 2003, she was deployed multiple times on training and humanitarian missions. When her army reserve unit was deactivated, to keep flying, she switched into the National Guard. In 2004 she was deployed to Iraq—a combat zone. As a battle captain, she planned and piloted heli-

While deployed to Iraq in 2004, Duckworth survived a grenade attack on her helicopter. She lost both of her legs. She spent thirteen months recovering in the hospital. During her recovery she underwent more than twenty surgeries and grueling physical therapy.

copter missions. On November 12, 2004, eight months into her deployment, the helicopter she was flying was hit by a rocket-propelled grenade, which detonated in Duckworth's lap. It blew off her legs, shattered her right arm, burned her skin, and riddled her with shrapnel, making her the first female double amputee of that war. She and her copilot miraculously landed the damaged aircraft, and the crew dragged her body to safety. She explains:

> My right leg was vaporized; my left leg was crushed and shredded against the instrument panel. My pilot in command miraculously brought down the helicopter safely. I went from being the most senior member on board to the weakest. I could easily have died that day, but my crew wouldn't give up on me. They pulled me from the disabled aircraft and, when help arrived, insisted I be attended to first even though some of them were also seriously injured.[28]

Alive Day

Every year on November 12, Tammy Duckworth celebrates what is known in the military as her "alive day." This is the name given to the anniversary date when veterans and military members who almost lost their lives in combat celebrate their survival and honor the memories of those who were not as lucky. On Duckworth's alive day she gets together to joke and reminisce with members of the crew who were with her when her helicopter was shot down and who valiantly saved her life. The group has held a reunion almost every year since 2005. According to Duckworth, "We get together once a year on 'alive day' to celebrate survival, to celebrate a new birthday. That day will be stuck in our minds for the rest of our lives. It can be a really sad day or it can be a really happy day, and we chose to make it a happy day."

Quoted in Jennifer Cragg, "VA Official Celebrates 'Alive Day' with Crew," DVIDS, November 10, 2009. www.dvidshub.net.

Duckworth was taken to an army hospital in Baghdad, then to a hospital in Germany, and finally to Walter Reed Army Medical Center in Washington, DC, where she woke up eight days later in excruciating pain. It felt like her body was on fire. The pain was the worst where her feet and legs had been. That phantom pain became a constant in her life. She spent thirteen months recovering at Walter Reed. During her recovery she underwent more than twenty surgeries, and she spent countless hours in physical therapy learning how to walk on titanium legs. Throughout her ordeal, she tried to stay upbeat. She insists, "You can choose to cry about it, and you can choose to be depressed for the rest of your life about it, but at the end of the day, I earned my injuries. . . . And I'm proud that I earned this. Because I earned it in defense of my nation."[29]

During her recovery and rehabilitation, Tammy's goal was to heal enough to fly again, but this proved to be physically impossible. Duckworth had lost more than her legs when she was shot down; she also lost her identity as a military pilot and was unsure of her purpose in life. Nevertheless, she continued serving in the Illinois National Guard until she retired as a lieutenant colonel in 2014—with a Purple Heart, a medal for being wounded in combat.

A New Identity

Many politicians visit the wounded at Walter Reed. During these visits, Duckworth became friends with Illinois senator Dick Durbin. She used her connection to Durbin to be a voice for other patients who needed help with problems concerning their medical and pay issues. Her advocacy for these troops so impressed Durbin that in 2006, he encouraged her to run for the US Congress so she could help veterans on a larger scale. Duckworth had never considered becoming a politician, but the idea that she could help improve the lives of others made her decide to run. The campaign was physically and emotionally challenging for Duckworth. Her opponent, Peter Roskam, flooded the media with vicious campaign ads denigrating her character and race. She narrowly lost the race by less than five thousand votes.

Shortly after the election, the governor of Illinois asked her to become the director of the Illinois Department of Veteran Affairs, and in December 2006 she took the post. Just as she started in the job, Bowlsbey was deployed to Kuwait, where he served for a year. During her husband's deployment, Tammy worked hard to improve the lives of Illinois vets. Under her leadership, she launched programs that improved veteran's mental health care and access to housing. In 2008 she joined the Obama administration as the assistant secretary of public and intergovernmental affairs in the US Department of Veterans Affairs. Her work there improved conditions for female, Native American, and homeless veterans, among other programs. But although she accomplished a lot, Duckworth believed she could have an even greater impact as a legislator.

So in 2012 she ran for Congress for a second time. Once again, the campaign was nasty. This time her opponent, incumbent Joe Walsh, disparaged her gender and her military service. His criticism did not go over well with voters. Duckworth won the election, beating Walsh by more than twenty thousand votes. She went on to serve in Congress from 2012 to 2016. She was

Duckworth walks up to speak at the 2016 Democratic National Convention. She ran for Congress and won in 2012, becoming the first Thai American and disabled woman to do so.

the first Thai American woman, as well as the first disabled woman, to do so.

During her time in Congress, Duckworth and Bowlsbey tried unsuccessfully to become pregnant. In 2014, after several courses of in vitro fertilization (IVF) treatments, she gave birth to her daughter Abigail. Her experience made her a strong advocate for women's reproductive rights. Two years later, Duckworth ran for the US Senate, representing Illinois. The campaign was brutal. This time, her opponent, Mark Kirk, attacked her heritage and her family's military history. Although Kirk was favored to win, Duckworth prevailed. She was sworn into the US Senate in January 2017, as her husband, daughter, and mother watched. She was re-elected to a six-year term in 2022.

In July 2017 Duckworth again became pregnant via IVF, and in April 2018 her daughter Maile was born. Duckworth was the first female double amputee to serve in the Senate and the first US senator to give birth while holding office. Shortly after taking office, she sponsored a resolution allowing senators to bring children under one year old into the Senate chamber to breastfeed. A day after its passage, she became the first senator to do just that.

An Inspirational Legacy

Duckworth's bravery, persistence, strength in overcoming misfortune, and devotion to public service have made her an inspiration to people everywhere. Throughout her life she has broken many barriers and dedicated herself to helping others. Her work in politics and government have opened doors for veterans, women in the military, needy families, mixed-race individuals, and physically challenged people. She has worked on legislation expanding health care, creating jobs, supporting social services, rebuilding infrastructure, and helping working-class families. And besides being a busy mother, wife, and senator, she volunteers at local food banks. As she told reporters in 2024, "While I can't fly combat missions anymore or help drag Soldiers from a burning Blackhawk . . . I will always keep using my current role—serving no longer from the cockpit but the Senate—to improve lives."[30]

"While I can't fly combat missions anymore or help drag Soldiers from a burning Blackhawk . . . I will always keep using my current role—serving no longer from the cockpit but the Senate—to improve lives."[30]

—Tammy Duckworth

Taylor Swift, Cultural Icon

Jirandy is a young woman who has been a devoted Taylor Swift fan—or Swiftie, as Swift's fans are known—since 2009. Swift's songs touch her personally, reflecting her own life experiences. And Swift's strength and kindness have guided Jirandy through good and bad times. Although they have never met, like most Swifties, Jirandy considers Swift a role model and a friend. She explains, "Taylor has always been an inspiration for me; she has been that friend that has always been there though her music, whenever I needed her. Her songs are my personal diary to my everyday; there is always a song for ANY moment. . . . Taylor is a role model—the perfect one, even when she is not trying."[31]

A Gifted Child

Taylor Alison Swift was born on December 13, 1989, in West Reading, Pennsylvania, to Scott Swift, a stockbroker, and Andrea Swift, a homemaker who formerly worked as a marketing executive. Her brother, Austin, was born three years later. The family lived on a Christmas tree farm in rural Cumru Township, Pennsylvania, relocating to their second home on the New Jersey shore in the summers.

Taylor was a precocious child. Almost as soon as she could talk, she began singing and making up stories. At age three, she sang Disney tunes to anyone willing to listen, and when she forgot the words, the little storyteller made up her own lyrics. She admits, "My parents have videos of me on the beach at, like three, going up to people and singing Lion

King songs for them. I was literally going from towel to towel saying, 'Hi, I'm Taylor, I'm going to sing, "I Just Can't Wait to be King", for you.'"[32] The little girl was full of imagination and creativity. By the time she was five, she was writing poetry, and she won a national children's poetry competition a few years later.

Although already a poet, Swift did not become a country music fan until she heard a recording by country artist LeAnn Rimes. She fell in love with the songs and, more specifically, the stories they told. She vowed that she too would be a country music artist and tell stories with her music. She asked her parents to buy her a guitar, which she learned to play. She also started taking singing and acting lessons, performing in school plays, community theater, open-mic nights, festivals, and karaoke competitions. She loved being onstage. By the time she was eleven years old, she had become a local celebrity.

Taylor Swift was a precocious child. Almost as soon as she could talk, she began singing and making up stories, and sang Disney tunes to anyone willing to listen.

"When I first started writing songs, I was pretty lonely. . . . I wasn't popular, and I didn't have many friends, and never knew where to sit at lunch, but songwriting became a release."[33]

—Taylor Swift

Taylor's life seemed perfect until her parents sold the farm in 1999, and the family moved to Wyomissing, Pennsylvania. Taylor did not fit in at her new school. Her love of country music and her local fame made her an outcast. She was shunned, mocked, and bullied by her classmates. Out of loneliness, she started writing songs. She wrote about her own experiences and feelings and what she imagined her classmates were going through. She recalls: "When I first started writing songs, I was pretty lonely. . . . I wasn't popular, and I didn't have many friends, and never knew where to sit at lunch, but songwriting became a release."[33]

Determination and Persistence

Swift continued writing songs and performing whenever and wherever she could. She sang the national anthem before twenty thousand people at a Philadelphia 76ers game when she was eleven years old, receiving enthusiastic applause for her efforts. Shortly thereafter, she recorded a demo CD of covers of four country songs. Determined to break into the industry, she cajoled her mother into driving her to Nashville, where the little girl personally submitted her CD to every record company on Music Row.

No one offered her a deal, but this did not stop her from pursuing her dream. She kept writing songs and performing everywhere she could. In 2003 she recorded a new demo CD featuring several of her original songs, including "American Boy" and "Lucky You." Upon hearing it, RCA Records offered her an artist development contract. This is an arrangement in which a record company agrees to develop an emerging artist's skills with the possibility of signing the artist to a recording contract in the future.

To help Taylor pursue her dream, the Swifts moved to Nashville the summer before Taylor entered her freshman year of high school. She made friends in her new school and had her first boyfriend that year. He was a senior who reminded Swift of country artist Tim McGraw. When the boy left for college, she cowrote her first single hit, "Tim McGraw," as a parting gift to him. It was one of a succession of songs about love and heartache, a theme that would pervade her work.

Not Just Another Girl Singer

Indeed, although Swift was just fourteen years old, news of her songwriting skills spread around Nashville. Sony/ATV, a music publishing label, invited her to be part of its songwriting team. Swift was proud of the songs she was writing, but RCA was not impressed. When her artistic development contract ran out, the company offered to extend it but refused to allow Swift to record her own songs. Although most aspiring artists would have grabbed the deal, the determined teen turned it down. She says, "I had so many songs I wanted people to hear, I didn't want to be on a record label that wanted me to cut other people's stuff. That wasn't what I wanted to be."[34]

Friendship Bracelets

Making, wearing, and trading friendship bracelets has become very popular with Taylor Swift fans all over the world. The activity is partially inspired by a line in Swift's song "You're on Your Own, Kid," which mentions making friendship bracelets. Fans wear and trade bracelets before, during, and after Swift's shows. The bracelets are made of beads and charms that spell out titles and lyrics of the artist's songs, as well as inside jokes among Swifties. Trading bracelets are symbols of peace, love, unity, respect, and responsibility. They also help Swifties recognize each other and make new friends. The bracelets unite the community and their love for Swift together. Both female and male fans sport the bracelets. And many individuals wear dozens at a time, with the bracelets stretching from their wrists up to their elbows. Fans often share their pictures of their creations on social media and post tutorials instructing others on how to make the bracelets.

Searching for a new label, Swift performed her original songs at a local café and invited all the contacts she had made in Nashville to attend. Scott Borchetta, a young music industry executive who was starting Big Machine Records, a new independent record company, heard her. He immediately offered Swift a recording contract that allowed her to record her own material. In 2005 the high school sophomore signed with the company and shortly thereafter recorded her first album, *Taylor Swift*.

From the start Swift took control of her career. She was involved in the album's production. And she used social media to promote herself and the record. She set up a Myspace page where she blogged, posted videos of herself, streamed some of her songs, and interacted with visitors to the page. This type of personal approach was unique to Swift, and it was very effective. Even before the album was released, she had cultivated a large fan base. Once the album came out, she ceaselessly publicized it. She hand carried the recording to hundreds of radio stations, appeared on talk shows, and toured throughout the country, while still attending high school through a homeschool program.

Megastar

Swift's efforts paid off. The album was a huge success. Swift's fans, who at the start of her career were mainly tweens and young teens, were obsessed with the stories her songs told. They related to the teenage artist's lyrics. Swift's stories were their stories, too. As Eliana, one such fan, explains, "When I was in school, I related to songs like 'The Outside,' because I always felt so out of place. Taylor's music . . . made me feel like there was someone out in the world that knows exactly how I feel and acknowledges me."[35]

"Taylor's music . . . made me feel like there was someone out in the world that knows exactly how I feel and acknowledges me."[35]

—Eliana, Taylor Swift fan

Taylor Swift sold 1 million copies. It yielded five hit singles and was nominated for the 2008 Academy of Country Music Album of

Swift has won fourteen Grammy Awards and made more number one albums than any female artist in history.

the Year. Swift was now a superstar. She received multiple accolades for the album, and even more for each succeeding recording. As a matter of fact, her second album, *Fearless*, was the best-selling album of 2009, making Swift the youngest artist ever to have a year's best-selling album. And "Love Story," the album's lead single, crossed genres, fusing country and pop music to become one of the first songs ever to top both country and pop music charts.

Devoted Cat Mom

Taylor Swift loves cats and has three: Meredith Grey, Olivia Benson, and Benjamin Button. Meredith and Olivia are Scottish fold cats, a breed that has cute folded-down ears. Benjamin is a ragdoll cat, a breed that has blue eyes and a fluffy coat. Swift adopted Benjamin after the homeless kitten appeared in the "Me" music video. He is the youngest of the trio. In 2023, when Swift was named *Time* magazine's 2023 Person of the Year, he appeared with her on the magazine's cover.

In fact, all three cats have become celebrities. Swift posts videos of them on her social media pages and references them in her songs. The cats have appeared in her music videos. In 2020 she featured the felines dressed in winter clothes on her holiday cards. Swift takes the felines on her tours and has a specially designed backpack with a little window in which she carries them. She is so fond of cats that she joined the cast of the movie version of *Cats* and attended a "cat school" to prepare for the role. Swift also donates to animal rescue charities and encourages her fans to do so.

Undeniably, Swift has always forged her own path. Her belief in herself has let her take risks and do things that other artists avoid. Unafraid to evolve her sound and reinvent herself, she transitioned from country music to pop in 2014 in her groundbreaking album, *1989*. She did not lose fans because of the change, but rather gained more admirers. With each new recording her popularity has grown, turning her into one of the most admired artists in the world. She has won fourteen Grammy Awards and made more number one albums than any female artist in history. In fact, she is the only living artist to have eleven albums on the Billboard 200 chart simultaneously.

Swift has tirelessly worked to achieve and maintain her status, performing at festivals, award shows, and sporting events and headlining seven concert tours. These concerts are visually stunning extravaganzas featuring dancers, special effects, pyrotechnics, levitating stages, and guest artists. When she is not performing, she is busy writing music and putting out albums. In addition, she has written soundtracks for films, self-directed and performed in music videos, and appeared in television shows and films, including *Miss Americana*, a documentary about her life. And she has done it all her way. When she hosted *Saturday Night Live* in 2009, she was the first host to write her own opening monologue, which she delivered as a comedic song.

Friends Forever

Throughout her career, Swift has stayed closely connected with her fans. This connection may be the key to her great success. Throughout popular culture history, many artists have gathered a loyal fan base, but few have been as large, supportive, and deeply connected to an artist as Swift's fans. According to a 2023 survey by market research company Morning Consult, 53 percent of American adults say they are Swift fans; of these individuals, 52 percent are women and 48 percent are men. The majority are millennials who grew up beside her, but Swift also has many fans among younger and older people. She boasts 283 million followers on Instagram, 33.8 million on TikTok, and 95.2 million on X.

Indeed, from the start of her career, she has used social media to develop a one-on-one, personal relationship with her fans. But the relationship is more than virtual: Like a true friend, Swift attends fans' weddings and bridal showers, visits hospitalized fans, sends fans cards and gifts, and helps them when they are in need. She has paid needy fans' rents, medical bills, and student loans, bought a home for a homeless fan, and purchased a service dog for an autistic fan, among many other acts of kindness. She also hosts groups of Swifties in her home for secret listening sessions of her albums and snacks of homemade cookies. To further intrigue them, she puts subtle references, riddles, codes, and hidden messages in her lyrics. Among Swifties, these cryptic teasers are known as Easter eggs. Swift's fans analyze every lyric for Easter eggs, trying to interpret their meaning and references.

All these actions have created a seemingly unbreakable bond between Swift and her fans. They are incredibly loyal to her. They

> “Fans are my favorite thing in the world. I’ve never been the type of artist who has that line drawn between their friends and their fans. The line’s always been really blurred for me.”[36]
>
> —Taylor Swift

have her back no matter what, because she has theirs. As she explains, “Fans are my favorite thing in the world. I’ve never been the type of artist who has that line drawn between their friends and their fans. The line’s always been really blurred for me. I’ll hang out with them after the show. I’ll hang out with them before the show. If I see them in the mall, I’ll stand there and talk to them for 10 minutes.”[36]

Businesswoman and Philanthropist

In addition to being one of the most popular and beloved musicians of all time, Swift is one of the richest. In 2023 Bloomberg News reported that she earned $1.1 billion, mainly through her music earnings. She has proved to be a clever businesswoman who is unafraid to stand up for her own rights and for the rights of other artists. For example, in 2015 she threatened to pull her music from Apple Music because it refused to compensate artists during the streaming service’s three-month free trial period for users. As she wrote in an open letter to the company, “We don’t ask you for free iPhones. Please don’t ask us to provide you with our music for no compensation.”[37] Less than a day later, the company complied by agreeing to compensate the artists.

She made an even bolder move in 2019 when Big Machine Records was sold and the new owner, Scooter Braun, gained control of her catalog. This gave him control of where and how all the songs on Swift’s first six albums could be used, as well as any future royalties they earned. Swift offered to buy back the catalog, but the new owner refused to sell. So, in an audacious act, she rerecorded her catalog on her own, thereby reclaiming control of her work.

Rerecording her catalog proved to be one of many savvy financial moves the confident businesswoman has made. She currently owns her own record label, music publishing company, and film and video production company. In 2023 she bypassed Hollywood studios and personally funded the making of her *Eras Tour* movie, which allowed her to receive more than 50 percent of the profits. "I did what I tend to do more and more often these days, which is bet on myself,"[38] she explains.

Swift has also created a powerful business and merchandising empire outside of the music industry. She invests in real estate and start-up tech companies. And she endorses a wide variety of products based on her values and image. She also collaborates with designers to create jewelry, dolls, fragrances, sustainable clothing, and greeting cards, among many other items. Her loyal fans are quick to purchase these products.

Swift is equally generous about sharing her tremendous wealth. In addition to helping needy fans, she quietly contributes to many charitable causes. For example, she donated to food banks in every city on her Eras concert tour. She also donates large sums to charities that support the arts, promote childhood literacy, advocate for LGBTQ rights, and help victims of sexual assault, child abuse, childhood cancer, and natural disasters.

One of the Most Powerful Women in the World

Her success as an artist and businesswoman, her philanthropy and acts of kindness, and the genuine connection she has with her fans have made Swift one of the wealthiest and most influential women in the world. *Forbes* reports that, as of October 2024, her net worth was $1.57 billion. Her concert tours bring as many as ninety-six thousand fans to each venue. Indeed, her Eras Tour was the highest-grossing concert tour ever. All 151 shows sold out, generating huge revenues for state and local economies. According to *Forbes*, just two nights of her Eras Tour shows in Denver added $140 million to Colorado's gross domestic product because of fans spending on food, hotels, and merchandise. Indeed, her presence anywhere is a boon. In 2023 when she started dating Kansas City Chiefs tight end Travis Kelce, sales of

Swift's Eras Tour was the highest-grossing concert tour ever. All 151 shows sold out, generating huge revenues for state and local economies and making her one of the wealthiest women in the world. Swift is shown here performing in Miami in October of 2024.

Kelce's jersey increased by 400 percent, and viewership of NFL games rose as much as 53 percent among females.

Swift's clout goes beyond economics. She is a cultural icon who is unafraid to use her platform to rally her fans to social causes she supports. In the process, she has raised awareness about social issues, influenced public opinion, and driven social change. In 2023, for instance, when she posted a short message on Instagram encouraging her fans to register to vote, more than thirty-five thousand people did so that very day. Her impact is so great that colleges throughout the world offer classes studying her writing, business acumen, and societal influence. There is little doubt that she will go down in history as one of the greatest music and cultural icons of all time. Nevertheless, she is still the same kind, generous person she has always been. As a matter of fact, she regards the way she treats others as her greatest achievement. "No matter what happens in life," she maintains, "being good to people is a wonderful legacy to leave behind."[39]

SOURCE NOTES

Introduction: Impacting the Lives of Others

1. Quoted in BBC, "Nadia Murad—from Rape Survivor in Iraq to Nobel Peace Prize," BBC, October 5, 2018. www.bbc.com.
2. Quoted in Rebecca Collard, "He Helped Nadia Murad Escape ISIS. Now He's Poor and Alone," *Time*, July 13, 2018. www.time.com.

Chapter One: Sylvia Acevedo, from Girl Scout to Rocket Scientist

3. Sylvia Acevedo, *Path to the Stars*. New York: Clarion, 2018, p. 114.
4. Acevedo, *Path to the Stars*, p. 104.
5. Quoted in Jessica Rosenworcel, "Girl Scout CEO Sylvia Acevedo," Federal Communications Commission, October 3, 2019. www.fcc.gov.
6. Acevedo, *Path to the Stars*, p. 232.
7. Acevedo, *Path to the Stars*, p. 252.
8. Quoted in Elissa Nadwarny, "From Poverty to Rocket Scientist to CEO, A Girl Scout's Inspiring Story," NPR, September 5, 2018. www.npr.org.
9. Quoted in Bruce Horovitz, "How Sylvia Acevedo Defied Barriers to Become Girl Scout CEO," *Investor's Business Daily*, April 11, 2024. www.investors.com.
10. Quoted in Rosenworcel, "Girl Scout CEO Sylvia Acevedo."
11. Quoted in Jim Cavan, "Sylvia Acevedo—Girl Scouts of the USA," *The Vision*, 2025. www.thevision-mag.com.

Chapter Two: Simone Biles, GOAT

12. Quoted in Simone Biles, *Courage to Soar*. Grand Rapids, MI: Zondervan, 2016, p. 23.
13. Biles, *Courage to Soar*, p. 41.
14. Quoted in Sporty Tell Editors, "50 Inspiring Simone Biles Quotes to Motivate You," Sporty Tell, April 5, 2021. www.sportytell.com.
15. Quoted in Biles, *Courage to Soar*, p. 157.
16. Quoted in Sporty Tell Editors, "50 Inspiring Simone Biles Quotes to Motivate You."
17. Quoted in Ally Mauch, "Simone Biles Opens Up About Experiencing Racism, Says Still Training 'as If' Olympics Will Happen," *People*, July 23, 2020. www.people.com.

18. Quoted in Abby Aguirre, "Simone Biles on Overcoming Abuse, the Postponed Olympics, and Training During a Pandemic," *Vogue*, July 9, 2020. www.vogue.com.
19. Quoted in Aguirre, "Simone Biles on Overcoming Abuse, the Postponed Olympics, and Training During a Pandemic."
20. Quoted in Brenley Goertzen, "Charlie Kirk, Piers Morgan Slam Simone Biles as a 'Selfish Sociopath' and 'Shame to the Country,'" *Salon*, July 28, 2021. www.salon.com.
21. Quoted in Anna Lazarus Caplan, "Simone Biles Embraces Being Called the G.O.A.T. Because 'It Makes People Happy and Just Pisses People Off,'" *People*, September 5, 2024. www.people.com.

Chapter Three: Tammy Duckworth, Guardian of Freedom

22. Quoted in Angela Nelson, "Tammy Duckworth: 'We're in a Fight for What America Is Going to Be,'" Tufts Now, November 19, 2021. www.now.tufts.edu.
23. Tammy Duckworth, *Every Day Is a Gift*. New York: Twelve Books, 2021, p. 55.
24. Duckworth, *Every Day Is a Gift*, p. 72.
25. Duckworth, *Every Day Is a Gift*, p. 80.
26. Quoted in Jocelyn Sears, "17 Things You Might Not Know About Tammy Duckworth," *Mental Floss*, May 15, 2023. ww.mentalfloss .com.
27. Quoted in Ed Forgotson, "Sen. Tammy Duckworth on Striving for 'That More Perfect Union,'" CBS News, March 28, 2021. www .cbsnews.com.
28. Tammy Duckworth, "What I Learned at War," *Politico*, July/August 2015. www.politico.com.
29. Quoted in Rebecca Nelson, "The Dark Humor of Tammy Duckworth, Iraq War Hero and Gun Control Advocate," *GQ*, September 29, 2016. www.gq.com.
30. Quoted in WICS/WCCU, "Duckworth Reflects on the 20th Anniversary of Her Alive Day," News Channel 20, November 11, 2024. www.newschannel20.com.

Chapter Four: Taylor Swift, Cultural Icon

31. Quoted in De Elizabeth, "13 Taylor Swift Fans Reflect on the 'Lover' Era and What It Means to Be a Swiftie," *Teen Vogue*, August 25, 2019. www.teenvogue.com.
32. Quoted in Michael Francis Taylor, *Taylor Swift: The Brightest Star*. Welbeck Abbey, UK: New Haven, 2021, p. 14.
33. Quoted in Ben Gilbert and David Rosenthal, "Taylor Swift (*Acquired*'s Version)," *Acquired*, January 23, 2022. www.acquired.fm.

34. Quoted in Taylor, *Taylor Swift*, p. 37.
35. Quoted in Elizabeth, “13 Taylor Swift Fans Reflect on the ‘Lover’ Era and What It Means to Be a Swiftie.”
36. Quoted in Joseph Nyamache, “90 Taylor Swift Quotes from Songs About Love, Graduation, and Life Lessons,” *Blog Lingo*, July 18, 2023. www.bloglingo.com.
37. Quoted in Country 97.5 Honolulu, “Taylor Swift Scolded Apple Music for Not Paying Artists, and Apple Caved,” 2025. www.975country.com.
38. Quoted in Annabel Gutterman, “‘I Bet on Myself.’ How Taylor Swift’s Deal with AMC Came Together,” *Time*, December 26, 2023. www.time.com.
39. Quoted in Nyamache, “90 Taylor Swift Quotes from Songs about Love, Graduation, and Life Lessons.”

Books

Kristen Anderson, *Who Is Taylor Swift?* New York: Penguin Young Readers Group, 2024.

Deborah J. Felder, *100 American Women Who Shaped American History.* Naperville, IL: Sourcebooks Explore, 2023.

Stephanie Loh, *Who Is Simone Biles?* New York: Penguin Workshop, 2023.

Ann McCallum Stats, *High Flyers: 15 Inspiring Women Aviators and Astronauts*. Chicago: Chicago Review, 2022.

Internet Sources

Zoe Adams, "How Many Grammy Awards Has Taylor Swift Won? What About Billboard Music Awards? A Full Look Inside Her Prestigious Awards Cupboard," Capital, September 12, 2024. www.capitalfm.com.

BBC 100 Women Portal, "BBC 100 Women 2024: Who Is on the List this Year?," BBC, December 3, 2024. www.bbc.co.uk.

Biography.com Editors, "Tammy Duckworth," Biography, May 7, 2024. www.biography.com.

Biography.com Editors et al., "Taylor Swift," Biography, October 18, 2024. www.biography.com.

Ashley Buhler, "If Simone Biles' Career Ended in Paris, Her Legacy Will Live On Forever," NBC, August 6, 2024. www.nbcolympics.com.

Natfluence, "Sylvia Acevedo," 2022. www.natfluence.com.

USA Today Network, "2024 Women of the Year," *USA Today*, February 29, 2024. www.usatoday.com.

Websites

Nadia's Initiative

www.nadiasinitiative.org

Nadia's Initiative is an organization Nadia Murad founded to fight human trafficking and the genocide of the Yazidi people. The website offers information about Murad's life, the work she does, the Yazidi people, and the work of the organization

Simone Biles
https://simonebiles.com
This is Biles's official website. It offers biographical information, photos and videos, links to her social media pages, and information about her sponsors.

Smithsonian American Women's History Museum
www.womenshistory.si.edu
The museum's website provides a wealth of articles, stories, and videos about a wide variety of inspirational women.

Sylvia Acevedo
https://sylviaacevedo.org
Sylvia Acevedo's official website provides information about Acevedo's life and an archive with links to articles, podcasts, videos, and interviews with and about her.

Tammy Duckworth: U.S. Senator for Illinois
www.duckworth.senate.gov
This is Tammy Duckworth's official website. It provides a biography, information, press releases, news, and videos related to her work in the Senate.

Taylor Swift
www.taylorswift.com
Swift's official website has photos, videos, information, clips of projects she has directed, and information about her tours.

INDEX

Note: Boldface page numbers indicate illustrations.

PICTURE CREDITS

Cover: Grindstone Media Group/Shutterstock

5: Alexandros Michailidis
9: Associated Press
16: MARK GARLICK/Science Source
17: Associated Press
20: DFree/Shutterstock
25: Cal Sport Media/Alamy Stock Photo
29: dpa picture alliance/Alamy Stock Photo
32: BONNIE CASH/UPI/Newscom
37: Abaca Press/Alamy Stock Photo
40: Gregory Reed/Shutterstock
43: A.PAES/Shutterstock
47: s_bukley/Shutterstock
52: MEGA/Newscom/CGMIA/Newscom

ABOUT THE AUTHOR

Barbara Sheen is the author of 116 books for young people. She lives in New Mexico with her family. In her spare time, she likes to swim, practice yoga, garden, cook, and read.